GIANTS
OF THE LAND

Written by

Q. L. Pearce

Illustrated by

Lisa Bonforte

CHECKERBOARD PRESS

NEW YORK

To Carol, Sy, Jody, and Jon…and Monterey, too
—Q.L.P.

To William and Nicole
—L.B.

Acknowledgments

I would like to express my thanks to the following scientists for their careful review of the manuscript and illustrations:

Michael Cunningham, Curator of Birds, Los Angeles Zoo
Harvey Fischer, Curator of Reptiles, Los Angeles Zoo
Brian Harris, President, Lorquin Entomological Society,
and Curator, Natural History Museum of Los Angeles
Theresa Prator, Curatorial Assistant, Los Angeles Zoo
Tony Valenzuela, Curator of Mammals, Los Angeles Zoo
—Q.L.P.

Published by Checkerboard Press, Inc.
30 Vesey Street, New York, NY 10007

CONTENTS

WHAT MAKES A GIANT A GIANT?

Think of a giant land animal. If you pictured a mighty elephant or an enormous rhinoceros, you are certainly correct. But there are other animals in the giant world that are not so obvious. For example, you might not be impressed by the size of a mouse, but you would be amazed to see a beetle the same size. Some living things that are small compared with humans may be giants compared with others of their kind. A beetle the size of a mouse could be called a "giant" because it is larger than other beetles.

Why are some animals giants? For one thing, large size protects many otherwise defenseless species from predators. A baby elephant may fall prey to a great cat, but only a few animals, particularly humans, would attack an adult elephant. Giant size can be beneficial to a predator such as the tiger, too, since it enables the tiger to hunt and capture large prey.

Being big also allows animals within a given area to take advantage of resources (such as food and water) that are not available to others. For example, in the open forests and grasslands of Africa, giants such as the elephant and the giraffe are able to eat leaves high in the treetops, far out of the reach of many smaller creatures. Even small land giants, such as the tarantula, can dominate their particular environments because of their large size.

Large size has its disadvantages, however. Animals such as the buffalo and rhinoceros lose body heat more slowly than smaller creatures. This can be helpful when the weather is cold, but when temperatures climb, these giants must spend much of their day cooling off at a water hole or resting in the shade.

Moreover, everything about a large animal must be "designed" for its great size. An animal's size affects its life span, the way it moves, the number of babies it may produce, how fast the young grow, and the amount of food it must eat each day. There are limits to how large certain animals can be, too. An elephant can grow to the size it does because of its particular body structure. Its sturdy, pillarlike legs, which are out of proportion to its body as compared to the legs of most other mammals, are specially designed to support the elephant's tremendous weight. But it would not be possible, say, for an ant to grow to the same size. There are several reasons for that. For one thing, an animal doubles in size (that is, doubles its height, length, and width), its weight doesn't just double but rather increases by about eightfold. An ant's hard outer covering (called an exoskeleton) works well enough for a creature of small size. It provides protection, and it has tiny openings in it that keep the animal cool and allow it to "breathe" air. But an ant the size of an elephant would probably overheat, die of lack of oxygen, and collapse under the heavy weight of its exoskeleton. So you can see, the monstrous insects that prowl across the screen in science fiction films are only make-believe!

Giants are found on all the continents on Earth, from the sunny grasslands of Africa to the Arctic's frozen plains to the outback of Australia. Giants even lurk on remote islands! As you read this book you will discover many animals that not only share a similar habitat or environment, but also, in one way or another, depend on large size for their survival. You'll also meet the record holders—those animals that, within a given giant species, grew well beyond the average size of their fellows. So turn the page and encounter giants of the land!

THE AFRICAN ELEPHANT

AT 25 FEET LONG, 12 FEET HIGH, AND WEIGHING 12,000 POUNDS, THE AFRICAN elephant is the largest and heaviest land animal on Earth. Its impressive ears can measure 6 feet from top to bottom, with a total spread of up to 20 feet from the outer tip of one ear to the outer tip of the other. When the weather becomes too warm, this enormous mammal gently fans its jumbo ears—which are laced with blood vessels—to cool the blood flowing through them. Both male and female elephants have a pair of enlarged teeth called tusks. Each tusk can weigh as much as 150 pounds and grow more than 11 feet long. The elephant also has a very long trunk, which it uses to gather grasses from the ground and fruit, leaves, and twigs from the treetops.

Record Holder

The largest elephant on record was a male discovered in Angola, a country on the western coast of Africa. It was 12 feet, 9 inches tall and more than 33 feet long. This behemoth weighed close to 24,000 pounds!

THE GIRAFFE

THE GIRAFFE IS THE WORLD'S TALLEST ANIMAL. A FULL-GROWN, 2,500-POUND male measures 18 to 20 feet from head to toe. The giraffe's height offers excellent protection from lions and other enemies: Not only does the animal have an excellent view of its surroundings, but also, because of its long legs and broad stride, it is usually able to outdistance predators at speeds of 30 miles per hour. Great height also enables this mammal to munch on tender leaves high in the treetops. What's advantageous for eating, however, is disadvantageous for drinking. To reach a water hole for a drink, the giraffe must spread its front legs wide, then lower its shoulders and head to the water. In this awkward stance it is at greatest risk of attack.

Fun Fact

A giraffe's brain is a full 10 feet above its heart. To pump blood that far, this giant's heart must be unusually big and strong. A human heart is about the size of a closed fist, or approximately 4 inches long. The giraffe's slender heart can be more than 20 inches long!

THE OSTRICH

THE WORLD'S LARGEST LIVING BIRD, THE OSTRICH ROAMS THE GRASSLANDS and semi-arid deserts of Africa. This 300-pound bird measures 6 feet from the tip of its strong beak to the end of its fluffy tail feathers, and it can be an astounding 9 feet tall. With its long neck it has no trouble reaching down to graze on grass and seed or to capture ground-dwelling insects and other small animals. The ostrich cannot fly, so it relies on speed to escape predators such as lions or cheetahs. But that's no problem for this huge bird—its strong legs enable it to run faster than any other two-legged animal—up to 40 miles per hour. These powerful legs also enable the ostrich to deliver a stunning kick when it is cornered.

Record Holder

The ostrich lays the largest eggs of any land animal. About 7 inches long and up to 6 inches wide, an empty ostrich egg can hold about 40 chicken eggs!

THE WHITE RHINOCEROS

THE WHITE RHINOCEROS OF SOUTHERN AFRICA IS SECOND IN SIZE ONLY TO the elephant. Weighing up to 8,000 pounds, its hefty body is more than 12 feet long and 5 to 6 feet high at the shoulder. A peaceful animal, the white rhino rarely charges, relying instead on its huge size to discourage possible predators. This rhino is not called "white" for its color (it's actually a dull gray), but rather for the Dutch word *wijde*, which sounds similar to "white." The word actually means "wide" and describes the white rhino's extremely broad, flat mouth. Because of its huge bulk, this mammal often seeks out water during the hottest part of the day. It bathes or wallows in the mud to prevent overheating and to get relief from biting insects.

Record Holder

Indricotherium (in-drik-oh-THEER-ee-um), an ancestor of the white rhinoceros that lived about 30 million years ago, is the largest land mammal that has ever existed. It was 26 feet long and weighed at least 5 times more than its descendant.

THE GOLIATH BEETLE

GOLIATH WAS A BIBLICAL GIANT KNOWN FOR HIS GREAT SIZE AND INCREDIBLE strength. The Goliath beetle of the African rain forest measures up on both counts. It is as much as 6 inches long and 4 inches wide—bigger than your hand! This beetle (a relative of the North American June bug) spends most of its time in trees. It is an excellent flier and zooms through the treetops on tough, leathery wings that are as wide as those of a sparrow. The male Goliath beetle has an upturned horn on its head, which it uses to dislodge or tip over rival males. The Goliath beetle feeds on the leaves and buds of various trees.

Record Holder

The amazing Goliath beetle is not only one of the world's largest insects, but it is also without doubt the heaviest, weighing more than one-quarter of a pound.

THE GORILLA

THE MIGHTY GORILLA IS THE HEAVIEST MEMBER OF THE PRIMATE ORDER, which includes lemurs, monkeys, apes, and humans. The huge but gentle male gorilla weighs about 500 pounds, or 3 times the weight of an average human adult male. When it stands on its hind feet, it can tower more than 6 feet tall. (Females, however, rarely exceed 5 feet tall and 200 pounds.) Under the protection of a dominant male, gorillas live in bands of 10 to 30 members. During the day the group browses together on fruit and leaves, taking turns gently grooming each other's fur.

Fun Fact

The gorilla is very intelligent and uses a wide range of sounds and gestures to communicate with other gorillas. In a remarkable project, scientists taught American Sign Language to a very special female gorilla named Koko, who can sign and understand hundreds of words.

THE AFRICAN BUFFALO

OF THE THREE SUBSPECIES OF AFRICAN BUFFALO, THE LARGEST ONE LIVES IN eastern and southern Africa. From head to tail, this sturdy mammal measures from 7 to 10 feet long, and its shoulder height is more than 5½ feet. It can weigh as much as 1,800 pounds. Gathering in herds of up to 2,000, these immense beasts graze on tough grass and never stray far from water. During the breeding season, large males have an advantage: When dueling for a mate, the biggest and strongest among them have the best chance of winning.

Fun Fact

The horns of the African buffalo (present in both males and females) are extremely heavy and wide set. On a sizable male, the sharply curved horns can be up to 3 feet long.

THE ELAND

THE MANY SPECIES OF ANTELOPE IN AFRICA DISPLAY A WIDE VARIETY OF shapes and sizes. The largest is the magnificent eland (EE-lund). These hefty mammals form herds of up to 200 members that mingle peacefully with herds of other antelope as well as zebras. The eland is 11½ feet long, stands 6 feet tall, and weighs 2,000 pounds. Although the female eland is smaller than the male, her horns are often longer than his and can grow to 3 feet in length. If a predator such as a lion threatens an eland calf, the calf's large, powerful mother can readily defend it. This strategy, typical of large animals, helps to ensure survival of the young.

Record Holder

Weighing in at just 9 pounds, the royal antelope, the smallest antelope of Africa, is 22 inches long and 12 inches high. The eland is nearly 6 times longer than its little relative and more than 200 times heavier.

THE HIPPOPOTAMUS

THE NAME *HIPPOPOTAMUS* IS GREEK FOR "RIVER HORSE." THIS MAMMAL LIVES in the lakes and rivers of Africa, spending up to 18 hours a day in the water. (Indeed, baby hippos are born in the water and learn to swim before they can walk.) When this creature submerges its 15-foot-long, 3- to 4-ton body, only its eyes, ears, and nostrils show above the surface. The hippo can stay underwater for 10 minutes or more before resurfacing. It even walks along the river bottom. The hippo can eat a whopping 250 pounds of grass and water plants a day. Its 10-foot-long stomach can hold nearly 6 bushels of plant matter at a time—enough to fill a shopping cart!

Fun Fact

The two front ivory teeth, or tusks, in a hippo's lower jaw measure up to 2 feet long and weigh about 9 pounds each. President George Washington owned a set of false teeth made from hippo ivory.

THE GOLIATH FROG

FOR MANY YEARS, NATIVES OF THE EQUATORIAL RAIN FORESTS OF WEST Africa told tales of a strange giant frog. They called it *niamona* (nee-uh-MOHN-uh), or "mother's son," and believed it looked like a newborn human. The 7- to 10-pound Goliath frog actually looks nothing like a human infant. It is, however, the world's largest frog, stretching a full 3 feet from nose to toe. The Goliath frog lives beside cool, fast-running streams or near pools widened by the erosive force of small waterfalls. It crouches on spray-dampened rocks, waiting quietly for suitable prey. Because of its size, this amphibian feeds not only on insects, but on other frogs and small rodents as well.

Record Holder

The world's smallest frog is the tiny Sminthillus limbatus (smin-THIL-us lim-BAT-us) of Cuba. This little creature is less than one-half-inch long. That's about 70 times smaller than the giant Goliath frog.

THE ANACONDA

THE ANACONDA OF THE AMAZON RIVER IS THE WORLD'S LONGEST, HEAVIEST snake. An excellent swimmer, this 20- to 25-foot-long, 200- to 250-pound reptile usually stays in or near water. The anaconda is not venomous; instead, it kills by constriction. First it wraps its muscular body around its prey. Then, each time the trapped animal exhales, the snake tightens its coils. Within minutes the victim suffocates. The anaconda can also drown its victims, as it can remain submerged for up to 10 minutes. Because of its huge size, the anaconda preys upon a wide range of creatures, from small lizards and turtles to mammals and birds. One anaconda killed a caiman (pronounced KAY-mun, a relative of the crocodile) nearly 7 feet in length!

Record Holder

The largest confirmed length of an anaconda is a little more than 37 feet. Although the specimen was not weighed, scientists calculate that it must have tipped the scales at many hundreds of pounds.

THE CAPYBARA

AT 4 FEET LONG, NEARLY 2 FEET TALL AT THE SHOULDER, AND WEIGHING UP to 200 pounds, the capybara (kap-ih-BAR-uh) is the world's largest rodent. This mammal lives in the forests and grasslands of South America, never far from water. A capable swimmer, the capybara spends a great deal of time in the water feeding on aquatic plants. Although it is the giant of its family, the capybara has several predators, including jaguars and humans (who both hunt it for its flesh). It can defend itself with its sharp, hooflike claws, but more often it relies on its numbers to discourage an attack: The capybara is the only rodent to gather in family herds of 15 to 20 individuals.

Record Holder

Many giants appear on the capybara's ancestral family tree. The largest, Telicomys (tel-ih-KOHM-eez), belonged to a group known as the "terrible mice" that lived about 5 million years ago. It was about the size and weight of a small rhinoceros.

THE GIANT ANTEATER

LARGEST OF THE ANTEATERS, THE ODD-LOOKING, SHAGGY-COATED GIANT anteater is nearly 7 feet long, but its bushy tail makes up more than one-third of that length. This mammal roams the South American grasslands, feeding on ants and termites. It usually hunts during the day, finding its food by scent. Its sense of smell is at least 40 times more sensitive than that of a human. Although the giant anteater is not aggressive, it is quite able to defend itself from its main predator, the jaguar. Because of its size, strength, and remarkably stout, sharp claws (the longest of which measures 4 inches), this anteater can inflict deep wounds on an attacker.

Record Holder

The giant anteater is toothless, but that doesn't stop it from gobbling down nearly 30,000 insects a day. This creature has the longest tongue (up to 2 feet long) of any animal and uses the sticky tool to gather up its meals.

THE GREATER RHEA

O F THE TWO VARIETIES OF THIS FLIGHTLESS GRASSLAND BIRD OF SOUTH America, the greater rhea (REE-uh) is the largest. The tallest bird on the South American continent, it towers 5 feet but usually weighs no more than 50 pounds. Powered by long, strong legs, the greater rhea usually relies on speed to escape its enemies. It runs from danger with its neck outstretched and one wing raised over its back like a sail. Rheas can be aggressive, however, and will defend their chicks against even large enemies. One male reportedly charged a small airplane that was landing near the spot where its chicks were feeding. Gathering in flocks of between 15 and 30 birds, greater rheas graze on roots, seeds, and grass, and feed on insects and small rodents.

Record Holder

The tallest land bird that has ever lived was a relative of the greater rhea. Called the moa (MOH-uh), it weighed about 900 pounds and was 12 feet tall, and became extinct about 700 years ago.

THE GIANT ARMADILLO

ARMADILLOS ARE UNIQUE IN THAT THEY ARE THE ONLY MAMMALS THAT HAVE a tough covering of "skin armor." The giant armadillo is the largest of these animals, growing as much as a yard long (with an extra 20 inches of armored tail) and weighing 110 pounds. This sturdy size, together with a strong armor, make for an effective defense against predators. Eleven to thirteen movable bands across the giant armadillo's back make the armor very flexible, allowing the creature freedom of movement. This slow-moving forest dweller has 100 teeth, but these are too weak to use for grinding, so the giant armadillo licks up ants, worms, and spiders with its sticky tongue.

Record Holder

The giant armadillo digs for its meals using the sharp—and amazingly long— claws on its forefeet. The longest of these strong, sickle-shaped claws grows up to 8 inches.

THE GIANT OTTER

T HE GIANT OTTER LIVES ALONGSIDE RIVERS AND LAGOONS, WHERE IT BUILDS a simple nestlike shelter of long grass or digs a burrow into the bank. The 5-foot-long, 65-pound giant otter is well suited to water; in fact, that is where this mammal spends most of its time. It has webbed feet and can dive to a depth of about 10 feet. It can also dart quickly through the water using its wide, flat, 28-inch-long tail. Giant otters usually gather in small groups and communicate through a wide variety of whistles, chirps, and sharp cries. Like other otters, this creature is playful. Through play, young otters learn and practice the hunting skills they need to survive.

Record Holder

The giant otter feeds on fish, birds, and small mammals. It eats about 9 pounds of food each day. For you to eat a similar amount compared to your body weight, you would have to consume about 9 to 12 pounds of food (as much as 24 plates of spaghetti) every 24 hours!

THE BRAZILIAN TAPIR

RELATED TO THE RHINOCEROS OF AFRICA, THE TAPIR (TAY-per) IS THE LARGEST land mammal of South America. Although it does not rival the rhino's great bulk, the Brazilian tapir still weighs a sturdy 500 pounds and is 6½ feet long and about 3 feet tall at the shoulder. The tapir, which usually lives in dense forests near water, is a good swimmer and diver. It spends most of the day in the water, tramping ashore at night to sleep on the riverbank. This shy mammal eats leaves and twigs, which it grips with its flexible snout. Its chief predator is the jaguar, but a full-grown tapir is an able match for the great cat.

Record Holder

The largest Brazilian tapir on record was a male that was an astounding 8 feet long. This enormous animal weighed about 550 pounds.

THE TARANTULA

ALSO KNOWN AS THE BIRD-EATING SPIDER, THIS ARACHNID IS SO HUGE IT would barely fit in the palm of your hand. Among the largest of the world's spiders, its body length is about 3 inches, and its total leg span is up to 10 inches. The tarantula prowls among the dead leaves on the floor of the Amazon River basin, hiding during the day and hunting at night. Because of its great size, it can capture and eat such large prey as mice, nesting birds, and even snakes. Although venomous, the tarantula's venom is designed to subdue rather than kill its victims. It rarely bites humans, even when handled. If threatened, however, it will rise up on its four hind legs and display its fangs.

Fun Fact

This spider does not chew its food. Rather, it injects a substance that liquifies the innards of its victim so it can "drink" its meal. The tarantula can dissolve and eat an entire mouse, bones and all, in just a day and a half.

THE KODIAK BEAR

T HE MASSIVE KODIAK BEAR IS THOUGHT TO BE THE LARGEST SUBSPECIES OF brown bear and the heaviest bear in the world. This giant mammal lives on a few scattered islands off the southwestern coast of Alaska. A grown male may be 10 feet long and weigh a staggering 1,800 pounds. It eats a wide range of foods, including berries, nuts, roots, insects, rodents, and fish, and it is capable of killing large prey if necessary. Size contributes to the Kodiak's ability to obtain and consume large amounts of food. This animal's weight, however, varies tremendously. By eating 80 to 90 pounds of food each day, a brown bear can put on 3 to 6 pounds in just 24 hours. This is extremely important because, while the Kodiak rests throughout the winter, it must rely on the 6- to 10-inch layer of fat stored under its skin to sustain itself until spring.

Record Holder

The brown bears of Kamchatka in the Soviet Union are said to be larger than the Kodiak. One scientist measured a track that was 15 inches long and 10 inches wide—the largest ever recorded. However, since a living Kamchatka bear has never been observed by scientists, the Kodiak still holds the title of largest brown bear.

THE GRAY WOLF

THE GRAY WOLF, THE GIANT OF THE DOG FAMILY, ROAMS THE FORESTS AND tundra of North America and Asia. It can be 5 feet long or more from its nose to the tip of its bushy tail and weigh up to 175 pounds. Gray wolves generally live and hunt in small groups, or packs, of 5 to 15 members. Organized by rank, each wolf pack has a very strict social order. The leader is the "alpha" male (meaning the "A," or first, male) and his mate is the dominant female. The pack members communicate through barks and yelps. Wolves will eat whatever they can catch, but they prefer large prey, such as white-tailed deer or caribou. A pack of wolves can even bring down such formidable prey as moose or bison.

Record Holder

The gray wolf has the largest natural range of any land mammal besides humans. Its range may cover from 25 to 115 square miles. When tracking its prey, a gray wolf can travel 40 miles without stopping.

THE MOOSE

THE GIANT OF THE DEER FAMILY IS THE MAGNIFICENT MOOSE. THIS 10-FOOT-long, 7-foot-tall beast is broad and stocky and may weigh up to 1,800 pounds. The moose lives in the open forests, bogs, and marshlands of the northern United States and Canada. It spends a great deal of its time grazing on aquatic plants, using the sensitive hairs on its bulky snout to find food in water. This mammal's great body holds in heat, helping the animal to stay warm during the harsh northern winters. However, its size does not always deter its enemies, which include powerful bears and wolves.

Record Holder

Only the male moose has antlers, and they are the largest of any animal—up to 7 feet across and weighing 60 pounds or more. The moose sheds its antlers in the winter and grows a new pair in the summer.

THE POLAR BEAR

THE POLAR BEAR IS NOT ONLY ONE OF THE LARGEST BEARS IN THE WORLD, but also the largest carnivorous land animal (which means it depends mainly on meat for survival). It can grow 8 to 10 feet long, not counting its stubby 6-inch-long tail. On all fours, this Arctic mammal is about 5 feet tall from shoulder to foot, and it can weigh as much as 1,500 pounds. Because of its large size, thick fur, water-repellent coat, and a substantial layer of fat under its skin, the polar bear is well suited to its icy world. It feeds on what it can catch, including walrus and fish, but it seems to prefer seals—specifically seal blubber. A capable hunter, this incredibly strong giant can kill its prey with one blow of its huge paw.

Record Holder

The largest polar bear ever recorded was a male more than 12 feet long that weighed over 2,200 pounds. The paws of this mammoth beast measured more than 12 inches across!

THE MUSK OX

THE MUSK OX, A CLOSE RELATIVE OF SHEEP AND GOATS, IS THE LARGEST grazing animal of the Arctic tundra. Individuals are between 6 and 8 feet long and about 5 feet high at the shoulder. The musk ox looks quite husky, but underneath its thick, warm coat, this mammal is rather slender and weighs no more than 675 pounds. Musk oxen travel in herds led by a dominant male. Since males battle for this honor, size is important and the largest, strongest bull usually wins.

Record Holder

The musk ox has the longest hair of any animal. Its dense coat, some 3 feet long, hangs down to its ankles. In winter this coat protects the musk ox from the cold, and in summer it provides protection from biting insects.

THE RED KANGAROO

T HE RED KANGAROO IS THE LARGEST ANIMAL OF AUSTRALIA. A FULLY GROWN male can weigh as much as 185 pounds and grow to a length of 9 feet from its long snout to the tip of its tail. Not only is the red kangaroo the largest Australian animal, it is also the world's largest marsupial (pouched mammal). Although being big helps to protect this animal from predators, it does have a drawback—large size makes it difficult for the red kangaroo to keep cool. Since it lives on dry, open grasslands, it must seek shade during the hottest part of the day. The red kangaroo becomes more active at night, when groups, called mobs, can graze comfortably on grass and plants.

Record Holder

The red kangaroo usually moves at a slow, easy pace. When alarmed, however, it can hop away at up to 40 miles per hour. It can jump higher and farther than any other two-legged animal, leaping more than 20 feet at a bound and springing over an obstacle as high as 9 feet tall.

THE GREATER GLIDER

ALTHOUGH NO MARSUPIALS CAN ACTUALLY FLY, SEVERAL VARIETIES DO TAKE to the air for short distances. Most are a few inches long and weigh only 3 or 4 ounces. The greater glider, however, is a giant among them. From head to tail, this animal is about 3 feet long. The greater glider lives high in the treetops of the eucalyptus forests of eastern Australia. By spreading the fur-covered membrane that is attached to its hindlegs and forelegs, this creature can float like a furry kite. It launches itself from the top of one tree, then sails out and down to grip the trunk of another tree nearby. There it runs straight up to the top and repeats the process, progressing easily from tree to tree.

Record Holder

The greater glider is able to cross distances of nearly 300 feet in one flight. The longest overall flight recorded was an astonishing one-third of a mile in six successive glides.

THE GAUR

DEEP WITHIN THE DENSE, DAMP FORESTS OF SOUTHEAST ASIA LIVE THE largest wild cattle on Earth. Known as the gaur (GOW-ur), this mammal has a combined head and body length of nearly 11 feet and may be 7 feet tall at its shoulder hump. The males, usually blackish or dark brown, are larger than the females, which have a coarse coat of reddish brown. In small herds numbering fewer than 10 individuals, the gaur feeds on grass and bamboo shoots that grow in jungle clearings. When approached by a tiger or other predator, healthy adult gaurs will usually come together to protect their young. This united front is generally enough to convince the intruder to retreat.

Fun Fact

The mating call of the male gaur—a powerful bellow—can be heard for up to a mile. This rumbling bellow will also be sounded at the sight of predators, including humans.

THE RETICULATED PYTHON

THE LARGEST SNAKE OF THE ASIAN CONTINENT IS THE UP-TO-30-FOOT-LONG reticulated python. Like the anaconda, the reticulated python kills by constriction; however, it is lighter and more slender than that close relative. Generally, the reticulated python eats rodents and small mammals, but it can entrap an animal as large as a 100-pound deer! For flexibility, its long backbone is made up of as many as 400 bones (the human backbone has a mere 33 bones). Powerful muscles enable this reptile to coil easily around its prey. Once this remarkable snake has eaten a large meal, it can go as long as a year before it eats again.

Record Holder

The largest reticulated python on record was measured at 32 feet, 9 inches long and weighed approximately 300 pounds. That's nearly twice the weight of an average human adult.

THE GIANT CENTIPEDE

THE AVERAGE GARDEN CENTIPEDE IS JUST A LITTLE MORE THAN 2 INCHES long, but the giant centipede of southeast Asia can reach an astounding 11 inches in length. A titan of the jungle floor, this creature, like other centipedes, is a predator. At night it ventures out, moving its 23 pairs of legs in alternating waves to feed on a variety of insects, and even toads and lizards. Just like all centipedes, the giant centipede is venomous. Its front legs are modified into claws that deliver a pinch designed to stun or kill its prey. Although not fatal to humans, this "bite" of the giant centipede is extremely painful. Its final pair of legs can also deliver a nasty pinch.

Fun Fact

For an insect, the giant centipede is a very attentive parent. The female gathers her eggs in a cluster and often wraps herself around them to protect them from predators and from drying out. She also licks them to keep them clean.

THE GIANT WALKING STICK

YOU MIGHT THINK THAT A GIANT WOULD FIND IT DIFFICULT TO HIDE, BUT THAT is exactly the strategy of the giant walking stick, the longest insect on Earth. Even though it may grow up to a foot long, it is very easy to overlook. During the day the giant walking stick remains quite still among the dense jungle vegetation. Because of its great length and brown or green coloration, it looks like a slender twig. To complete its masquerade, this giant insect sometimes sways slightly as if being blown by the breeze. At night it moves slowly among the branches of the rain forest, feeding on tender leaves.

Record Holder

The largest giant walking stick on record was a 13-inch-long individual discovered in Southeast Asia. Perhaps it would be more accurate to call that colossal insect a walking branch.

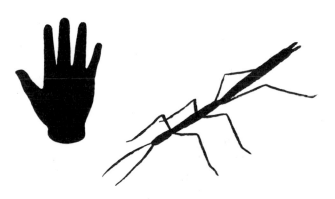

39

THE SIBERIAN TIGER

THE SIBERIAN TIGER IS THE GIANT OF THE CAT FAMILY. THIS MIGHTY CAT OF Asia can be more than a yard tall at the shoulder and 9 feet long, with its flashing tail adding nearly 3 feet. At up to 600 pounds, this mammal hunts mainly deer and can devour 90 pounds of meat in a single meal. Four-inch-long claws and three-inch-long stabbing teeth are the powerful weapons of this muscular giant. The Siberian tiger roams the oak forests of Manchuria and Siberia, although it is quite rare (less than 200 animals are known to exist in the wild). Well suited to its snowy environment, this tiger's large size and its thick, striped coat (which is paler than that of its southern relatives) help to retain body heat.

Record Holder

The largest Siberian tiger on record weighed 620 pounds. It was about 9¼ feet long (not counting its tail) and stood 44 inches high at the shoulder.

THE GIANT PANDA

WITH TINY, ROUND EARS, BLACK PATCHES AROUND ITS EYES, AND A FULL, FURRY belly, the giant panda looks like a cuddly stuffed toy. Scientists once debated whether this animal belonged to the bear or raccoon family, or perhaps even to its own family. Special tests, however, now prove that the giant panda is indeed a highly specialized bear. This animal measures about 5 to 6 feet long from its nose to its stubby tail and weighs a hefty 300 pounds or more. The giant panda lives in remote, misty bamboo forests in the mountains of Tibet and western China, where it munches up to 80 pounds, or more than 3,000 stems of bamboo a day.

Record Holder

The heaviest giant panda ever discovered weighed a portly 400 pounds. An animal of that size probably consumed 10,000 pounds or more of bamboo every year.

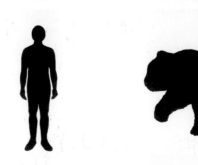

THE WILD YAK

THE LARGEST KNOWN MOUNTAIN DWELLER OF THE HIMALAYAS IS THE 10-FOOT-long, 1,200-pound wild yak. For centuries this animal has been widely tamed and is a great aid to humans. Not only is its milk a mainstay, but the surefooted yak serves as a trustworthy pack animal on treacherous mountain trails. The wild yak is generally larger than the domestic yak, its cousin. It has longer legs, bigger horns, and may weigh close to 1,800 pounds. In summer, this huge mammal grazes on grass in the high moors, and in winter it survives on moss and lichens scraped from icy mountain slopes. Large size and a dense, coarse coat of fur help the wild yak to survive in the incredibly harsh conditions of its habitat.

Record Holder

An expert climber, the wild yak lives at elevations of between 13,000 and 20,000 feet. No other Asian giant can live at as high an altitude. The yak is so well suited to the cold that it could not survive in a warmer climate.

THE GALÁPAGOS TORTOISE

O N SOME OF THE TINY, RUGGED GALÁPAGOS ISLANDS OFF THE COAST OF Ecuador, giant tortoises (among the largest in the world) were once so common that people claimed they could walk from one shell to another without setting foot on the ground. Hunting by humans has cut their numbers tremendously and only a small number remain. These creatures are the Galápagos tortoises, and there are several subspecies of them. The largest of these reptiles measures up to 50 inches in length and can exceed 600 pounds in weight. The diet of the Galápagos tortoise depends on which island is its

Record Holder

If undisturbed, the Galápagos tortoise has one of the world's longest life spans. It is estimated that this remarkable reptile may live to 175 years of age or more.

home, and the shape of a tortoise's shell is a clue as to what the animal eats. Tortoises with a slightly raised dome shape at the front of their shells dine on ground-level vegetation, including cactus. Those with tall, saddle-shaped openings at the front of their shells are able to raise their necks to reach low-growing tree branches.